UP CLOSE

Monster Trucks

PAUL HARRISON

Published in 2008 by Franklin Watts
Reprinted in 2010

Copyright © 2008 Arcturus Publishing Limited

Franklin Watts
338 Euston Road
London NW1 3BH

Franklin Watts Australia
Level 17/207 Kent Street
Sydney NSW 2000

Author: Paul Harrison
Designer (new edition): Silvie Rabbe
Editor (new edition): Fiona Tulloch

Picture credits: Alvey and Towers: page 14, top and bottom, page 20; Andrew Fielder: front cover, title page, page 4, top and bottom; Monster Photos: page 7, page 8, top and bottom, page 9, bottom right, page 10, top and bottom, page 11, page 12, page 17, top, page 18, top and bottom, page 22, page 24; Rex Features: page 16; page 21 photograph by kind permission of Liebherr.

A CIP catalogue record for this book is available from the British Library

Dewey number: 629.224

ISBN: 978-1-4451-0132-3
SL000945EN

Printed in China

Franklin Watts is a division of Hachette Children's Books, an Hachette UK Company
www.hachette.co.uk

Contents

Meet the

With their huge wheels and decorated cabs, monster trucks look like nothing else on the road. But whose idea was it to first make their truck look like that?

IN THE BEGINNING

Monster trucks were first created by Bob Chandler. He attached some extra large tyres to his pick-up truck so he could use it *off-road*.

Monsters

BIG THREE

The first makers of monster trucks were Ford, Dodge and Chevrolet. These were the big names of the business. They realised that there was a lot of money to be made from the trucks.

RULES AND REGULATIONS

Monster truck racing is now a sport with lots of rules and regulations.

BIGGER IS BETTER

People started competing over who had the biggest wheels. Huge wheels made the trucks even taller!

There is an official Monster Truck Racing Association.

TV TRUCKERS

Monster trucks are very popular in America. The television show *Monster Wars* showed trucks painted to look like superheroes!

GROWING POPULARITY

Monster Truck racing tournaments now take place all over the world, including Sweden and Australia.

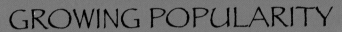

In *freestyle* competitions, trucks jump over cars, vans or even caravans!

Under the Skin

M onster trucks today are expensive, state-of-the-art machines. They are specially designed to cope with their unusual and demanding tasks.

BODY SWAP
The truck bodies are just one big piece of *fibreglass*. This means they can be moulded into wacky shapes. It also means that the doors don't open—drivers have to climb in through a trapdoor!

CAGED IN

A cage of strong
bars on the outside of the
truck stops it from getting crushed if it rolls over.
These bars protect the driver too.

WHAT A WHOPPER

Monster trucks weigh
around 4500 kg and can
travel up to 130 km per
hour. This means they
need large engines and a
special mix of alcohol
and fuel to run properly.

TALL TYRES
In 2002, Bigfoot 5 made it into *The Guinness Book of Records* as the world's biggest pick-up truck. It had 3-metre tall tyres.

GETTING SUSPENDED
Drivers need a soft landing after all those big jumps! Normal cars have spring *suspension*, but monster trucks have gas-filled tubes.

Monster trucks have four-wheel steering. This is handy for turning round in tight places.

9

Crushed

M onster trucks are known for doing bad things to other vehicles and for the long distances they can jump.

STAR ATTRACTION

In the early days, people wanted to see what else monster trucks could do. Driving over things seemed like a good idea! They became famous for crushing cars.

GOING UP, COMING DOWN

Driving over cars wasn't enough. Ramps were added for even more fun!

JUMPING FOR THE RECORD

Bigfoot 15 made a world record jump over a 727 airliner—a length of 61.5 metres. Black Stallion made a record jump measuring only 21 metres, but the driver was going backwards at the time!

The cars used in monster truck shows come from local scrap yards.

SAFETY FIRST

Drivers must wear helmets, safety harnesses, firesuits and head *restraints*. Trucks have switches in three places so that the engine can be switched off easily if they roll over.

PAINFUL

Big jumps can damage a monster truck's frame, but they are usually quite quick to fix. A driver's injuries are not so easy to repair.

The driver Dennis Anderson broke his kneecap, ribs and hands during his racing career.

Mud Glorious Mud

A lthough smashing up old cars was fun for a while, a new challenge was needed. Mud bogging and sled-pulling was the answer. It got messy!

MUCKY DEVILS

Mud racing, or mud bogging, is a sprint down a muddy track to a finish line. Those big wheels spin through the mud making dirt go everywhere!

A HEAVY LOAD

Sled-pulling was originally a competition between farmers and their tractors. To make the sled heavier, people would jump onto it as it passed. With monster trucks, weights are used instead of people.

PERFECT MIX

Mud bogging events require the perfect mix of soil and water. If it's too wet, the vehicles will sink as if in quicksand. Very dangerous!

NO SNOW REQUIRED

The sleds used are just like heavy trailers. The aim of the game is to see how far the truck can drag the sled along the straight line course. The truck that gets the farthest is the winner.

If a truck hits the mud at the right speed it can sometimes zip across the top.

15

Famous Trucks

When trucks started to compete against each other, they began to attract their own fans. People picked their favourites. The trucks soon became stars. Here are some of the really famous ones.

BIG DADDY

Bigfoot is the first and best monster truck. It has been adapted and improved seventeen times! There is even a Bigfoot that has been built like a tank with tracks.

MOULDED MONSTER

Samson has two huge arms extending from the cab. It is named after the man from the Bible with superhuman strength.

GIRL POWER

There are some women who are just as good at driving trucks as men. Madusa, an ex-wrestler, already holds a couple of championship titles.

JUNKYARD GENIUS

When Dennis Anderson built his scrap metal truck, he warned his competitors: "I'll take this old junk and dig your grave!" His truck was nicknamed "Gravedigger".

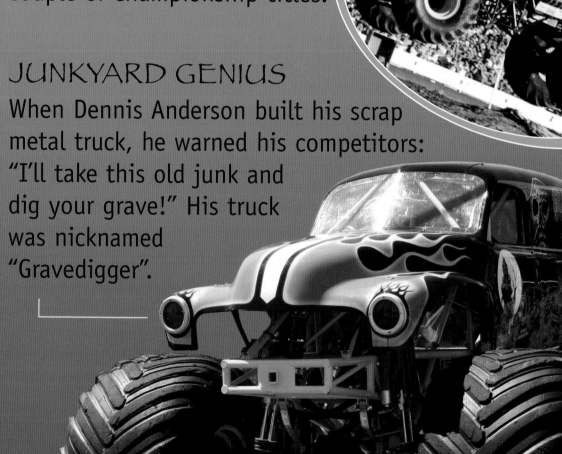

Puttin' on a

A monster truck show is a lot of fun—it's like nothing else you'll see. No other sport can combine jumps, crashes, fire—and, of course, lots of monster trucks!

LETTING RIP!

A monster truck show is called a *jamboree*. In the freestyle section, drivers can do things like burnouts. This is when the back wheels spin really quickly but the truck doesn't move.

ROBOT MAYHEM

At shows, cars are destroyed by even bigger monsters! Robosaurus picks up cars and pulls them apart with its teeth.

18

Show

Monster trucks are not allowed to drive on normal roads.

WARMUP ACTS

Small shows keep the crowd happy until the star act begins. Sometimes it is a demolition derby where old cars race around a track and smash into each other!

SELL, SELL, SELL

A jamboree is also a good time for people to get together and buy and sell things, from hot dogs to gigantic spare wheels!

The Monster

After seeing how popular monster trucks became, other machines were soon given the monster treatment.

MONSTER TRACTORS

These are your average farm tractors—times a hundred! They can weigh up to 3,600 kg. They have some of the biggest engines ever seen on land.

Bigfoot 5 is the world's biggest monster truck at 4.7 metres high.

READY FOR ANYTHING

The first *all-terrain* vehicle—called an ATV—was built in the 1970s. Early models had three wheels. This was increased to four and was called a quad bike.

Treatment

MINI MARVELS

If you're not old enough to drive, you could always try a radio-controlled mini-monster. They can travel at over 70 km per hour and do amazing jumps.

THE REAL MONSTERS

The biggest trucks are found in the mining industry. They have to move lots of earth and rubble, so the bigger the truck, the quicker they can do their job.

Glossary

ALL-TERRAIN
Something that can be driven over all different types of land.

FIBREGLASS
A strong material made from fine glass fibres, used for car bodies.

FREESTYLE
When a competitor is allowed to use whatever style he or she chooses.

JAMBOREE
A large gathering involving shows, speeches and entertainment.

OFF-ROAD
Not on normal roads—usually meaning uneven, rocky ground.

RESTRAINTS
Something that keeps someone safe and under control.

SUSPENSION
The springs that connect the wheels to a car's frame, to absorb shock.

Further Reading

Monster Jam: The Amazing Guide
James Buckley, DK Publishing, 2001

**Monster Trucks
(500 Series)**
Scott Bryant, Crestline, 2005

**Monster Trucks
(Mean machines)**
Sarah Levete, Raintree Publishers, 2005

**Monster Trucks
(Mighty Movers)**
Sarah Tieck, Buddy Books, 2005

**Monster Trucks
(Pull Ahead Books)**
Kristine L Nelson, Lerner Publishing
Group, 2002

Index